inspired by love

Love is a dictionary full of everything.

Poetries, Artworks and Quotes by Sharlene Leong

wordYourstory®
design. words. music.

Dearest Bep!
Hope you enjoy this
book of mine! :)
♡ Sharlene 2019

inspired by love
Copyright © 2016 by Sharlene Leong

Words, Design and Artworks by Sharlene Leong

Published by Word Your Story
www.wordyourstory.com

ISBN 978-981-11-1880-7

First Edition: November 2016
Special Cover Edition

Printed in China

10 9 8 7 6 5 4 3 2 1

Original Artworks Featured in this Book:
Medium: Acrylic Painting & Inked Quotes
Size: 92cmW x 46cmH x 4cm Thick Canvas

Cleanse Your Soul

Kisses Sensations

The Higher Power

Precious Memories

Feel Love

Authenticity

Embrace Imperfection

The Unknown

Have Faith

Butterflies

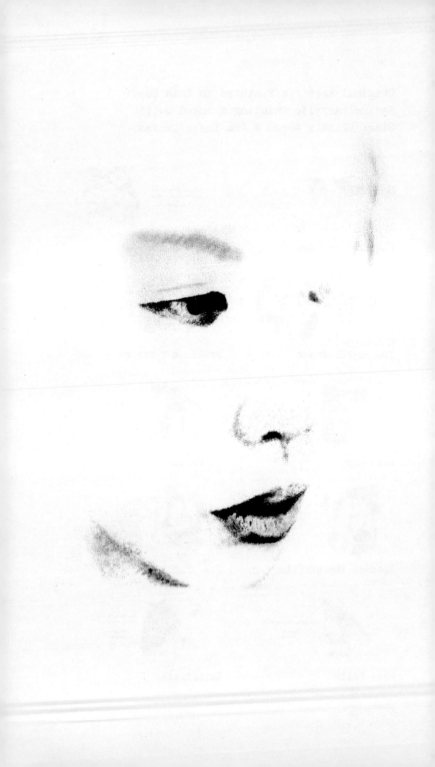

Dear Reader,

As words play a major part in my life,
It entices me with the power it possesses,
and morphs around the ideology of love.

Besides the physical and mental emotions attach to love,
feelings, stories and experiences are expressed,
through poems, imagery and reflective thoughts.

Pause, reflect, ponder and relate,
that love is a dictionary full of everything,
leading into never ending stories,
in the minds of the individuals.

Yours truly,
Sharlene Leong

JUST BE

Be open. Be nice.
Be alive. Be good.
Be free. Be easy.
Be sweet. Be kind.
Be opposite. Be in-between.
Be loved. Be around love.
Be heartwarming. Be grounded.
Be kissable. Be romantic.
Be helpful. Be memorable. Be amazing.
Be trustworthy. Be knowledgeable.
Be friendly. Be silly.
Be playful. Be childlike.
Be funny. Be forever young.
Be strong. Be vulnerable. Be wise.
Belong. Be there. Be present.
Be without enemies. Be careful.
Be happy. Be healthy.
Be YOU. Just Be.

The
energy
of existence
operates in
operates in
parallel order
to stay
on track
with
the universe.

YOU & I

A letter so important,
it meant nothing to you.
The deepest regret,
knowing we would never say hi.

You walked in my directions,
as you followed them all.
I remembered your routines,
as I followed them all.

You sat in front of me,
looked straight into my eyes.
I wrote you a note;
it never left the tight grip of mine.

You shied a little away,
noticed me noticing you.
I admired from a far,
yet dying to be closed by.

You saw me at your graduation,
without saying hi.
I left with a heavy heart,
as the courage left me by.

You picked up my call,
did not understand much of me.
I said, "I will email you",
trembled myself off the line.

You did not reply,
as you must have misunderstood me.
I wrote I would like to know you,
instead of I really like you.

You said nothing to me,
except not interested in knowing me.
I knew I said it all wrong,
I should have told you how I truly felt.

You picked up my call again,
asked if I have anything else to say.
I flew over to look for you;
I wanted to be part of your birthday.

You picked up my call one last time,
told me not to call anymore.
I wished you could be honest,
but you said you didn't know a thing or two.

You left without a word,
to fill that empty hole of mine.
I cried every night,
the pain that lasted seven years.

You never say you loved me,
not even hi.
I wrote the letter of you and I,
which left us behind.

Why live
only in regret,
if you know
what will flourish?

Go for it
if your heart says
it's worth it.

If silence
is the beauty
of it all,
embrace it
with peace.

You may have
lost in love,
but you have
become a lot wiser.

sharlene
wordYourstory
2016

Wipe those tears as they have cleansed your soul.

Sharlene Leong
Born 1980

WITH THE FLOW

Love takes two hands to clap,
instinct tells you when to clap.
The inner voice speaks,
the light within glows.

What is worth it,
yet it doesn't matter?
What is right,
yet what is wrong.

Go where the flow leads to,
for hearts will gel as one.
Answers are just answers,
no one can predict with wishes.

What are lies,
yet no truth really matters?
What are our responses,
yet we are our reactions?

Follow your dreams,
and move them into actions.
Confusion surrounds love,
let love summons connection.

Doesn't mean it is;
yet it shall be the way it is.
There will always be rules,
yet never stumble on rules.

You can never spell it all out,
yet it craves to be predictable.
Treasure while you can,
never go against the flow.

There is a reason
why they call it the flow,
it also means
being in the zone,
allowing things to unfold.

Without the
distraction of the emotions,
you flow along
with the momentum.

KISS

Longing for each other,
we walk home.
Photos we snap,
a kiss I sneak on your cheek.
We snuggle by the bench;
I lift your chin kissing your lips.

The rain pours,
for shelter we rush.
With your brolly,
there I shall leave.
Minutes pass like seconds,
where we embrace not to part.

The irresistible gaze in your eyes
shines through my heart.
There in the lift,
your lips touch mine.
Butterflies love,
cuddles and kisses unify us as one.

Treasure moments that will not last elsewhere,
but a lifetime in your heart.

Engrave memories that are real,
to stay forever sweet in your heart.

*Kisses are affections that leave
physical and mental sensations.*

*Sharlene Leong
Born 1980*

charlene
wordYourstory
2016

BEAUTY

The beauty through your eyes,
your glances sparkle bright.

Believing what was real,
I took my chances.

So close so soon,
you took me for granted.

So near so engaged,
yet it felt different.

There is no perfect timing for anything,
yet you got to know one to truly love one.

The true beauty of love begins only
through true colours of being.

YOURSELF

Leave desperation alone,
to discover yourself first.

Bask in the sweetness of the smile,
but not to overindulge you.

Find out the truth,
preventing you from a fantasy.

Protect yourself moving forward;
accept the facts being the truth.

Understand yourself,
accept yourself,
release yourself,
and detach yourself.

Don't dwell.

BETWEEN OUR VEINS

Memories sip deep between our veins,
from our private minds we refer to.

So real so sweet,
take breathes far away.

I fall in love,
dreaming you are with me.

You fall in love,
wishing I am with you.

Tears flow freely,
as sadness becomes our priorities.

Happiness will not last,
as promises do not last.

Our love so strong,
our wounds cut deep.

Our body so weak,
our traumas burn deep.

Lock our hearts,
the tears run dry.

Say you love me,
I do.

When
there is
nothing
you can
literally do,
no longer
try doing
anything.

Time through the higher power
heals all memories that burn.

Sharlene Leong
Born 1980

sharlene
word Yourstory
2016

NEVER

Never stop loving and missing yourself first.
Never miss someone so much that you lose control.

Never get lost in someone else's dream but your own.
Never forget the moment of truth.

Never seek a bad break but reconciliation.
Never stay true to the unreal but the real.

Never push yourself to the limits of
getting hurt before saving you.

Never search so hard for answers.
It is only a momentary need.

Never try so hard to get someone else's approval.
You know it's your own that matters.

Never think taking the blame will solve all problems.
It will literally not.

Never act tough when you feel soft inside.
Never lose yourself.

MOVING FORWARD

Don't be so sure about a statement made.
You might digest it the wrong way
with your perceive ideology.

No one will remember what went wrong,
but they will always remember the emotions
you made them feel.

Time passes; things change,
breathe the moments but always progress forward.

Discover a sense of determination,
with the right flow,
moving towards a destination.

ATTRACTION

Hearts collided,
attractions built.
You grew on me,
an email a day to you.
Our hearts bonded,
weakness we indulged.

Each time I thought of you,
smiles filled the air.
Our hearts grew fonder,
as we watched the fireworks.
Our love blossomed,
on the only moon.

Time passed,
you strangely detached.
Answers were only answers,
reasons never valid.
Questions avoided,
apart we drifted.

I searched for you,
each time I failed.
There were tons of reasons,
why I lost it.
I bleed and pleaded for us,
before him I prayed.

During your most difficult period,
devastation set in.
The truth could hurt;
yet not knowing was a torture.
Assuring you I would stop,
as it tormented you twice as much.

Pointless and worthless,
I chose to believe.
What was worth it,
I wouldn't even care.
A divine miracle,
I had been praying for.

Being swept away could be
a blessing in disguise,
yet it was believing
that needed strength.

The more you know,
the more you yearn
to find out even more.

TRUST

Trust that intuition of yours
that someone likes you.
Don't play games to find out.

Honestly,
there won't be a perfect
timing for anything.
Just go with the authentic flow.

When something happens,
trust in its goodness
that it is for the better.

Never deny the true feelings
that might never return real.

Enjoy the moment of truth
before the next moment arrives.

INSIDE OUT

Yes beauty could sometimes say it all,
but it should always
be discovered from the inside out.

When you made the same mistake twice,
you knew you allowed it to happen.

Don't deny it,
but reflect on it.

Be honest,
if you were not blinded by looks,
you would not fall for tricks.

Don't be blinded,

Learn to see beyond
the outer human shell,

HAPPINESS

You are important to me;
let it be of no consequences.
We are in love,
be glad it happened.
The future is unpredictable,
wait for its arrival.
Stay in laughter,
and indulge in the happy tears.

There are no reasons, no whys,
let nature takes its course.
Choose not to know,
there is always a reason to be unfolded.
Even if you know,
you should let it go.
What naturally lives,
has to naturally fade in time.

Trust in the higher power,
when you think it belongs to another.
If it ever hurts,
save yourself before you bleed.
When you do not have a choice,
it is already a choice made.
Always allow yourself to grow,
investing greater love and devotion.

Feel the power of love;
be contented in its existence.
Write the song in your heart;
fill it up with beautiful lyrics.
Be in the state of happiness,
a place without worries and doubts.
Embrace delightful memories,
to truly stay forever young.

charlene
wordYourStory
2016

*Cherish precious memories that
will never tarnish.*

Sharlene Leong
Born 1980

WHY

Why search to fill the hole?
Stop searching,
it will appear.

Why feel afraid yet act brave?
Keep close and bond.

Why hide in the corner,
yet yearning to reach out?

Be truly authentic,
you will be adored.

Welcome simplicity.

Reasons are just judgments.

Enjoy the lightness of it all.

Stay with happiness.

THE PATIENT ONE

Saw you in the club,
wasn't drawn to you like I would.
You were with another,
the more I wouldn't intrude.
We went for supper,
as friends teased us being eligible.

I knew why,
I did my thing again.
We chatted like pen pals,
moving quickly forward.
I thought you were attached;
yet you never knew.

Similarities in life,
we bonded as one.
The cracks appeared,
somewhere, out of the blue.
Sweetness turned into bitterness,
you easily strayed.

You took me for granted,
like most people did.
You treated me like,
I was just one of them.
You were externalising,
and I guessed I was too.

Hurt grew stronger,
yet ironically I loved you more.
No longer was I available to myself,
I chose to let you go.
You woke me up,
from a fantasy I was in.

I bided away,
till feelings faded into dust.
You called me up,
to spend the weekends, as friends.
Believe me,
those were the best three nights we had.

I clarified;
you said nothing leaving it as that.
We knew,
and that should be the end of our fate.
I remembered,
the day you said I was the only patient one.

Defining
something
might
stop
the flow of
undefined
magic.

Believe
in the
unknown;
let it
reveal itself
without over
exploring it.

TOO YOUNG

Young and beautiful,
this was you.
Trilling and fun,
we caught each other's eyes.
Not to appear desperate,
you were just too young.
Conversing so much,
we were engrossed.

Stuff I shouldn't hear,
you told me loud and clear.
Too young for an age like yours,
this was outraged.
Protect your youth my dear,
it should last forever.
You could tell I liked you;
you lured that out of me.

You never got close like that,
with someone like me.
Resisting you was my aim,
towards a young age, like yours.
The way you initiated a good night kiss,
seduced me high.
I felt it real,
I really did.

The next morning,
you became a stranger I never knew.
You did it on purpose,
to shut that door on me.
We had fallen fast,
when we knew it wasn't right.
This was unlike me,
I only said, "I will miss you".

You asked me what was wrong,
and said, "1 miss me too".
College would be your next path to take,
so we should really part ways.
I was never your destiny;
let us not play with fire.
Let us await our fate,
which was the best we should do.

Don't get into
a relationship
just because.

If you feel
something
is not right,
it is not right.

When you know
it is better to leave,
do it gracefully.

Trust in fate,
your future waits.

PROMISE

I laid eyes on you,
love at first sight I knew.
I treasured the little things we did,
even the split-second calls.
I waited for your meet up,
which was worth waiting for.

I loved the simplicity about you,
loving you being you.
I loved your direct words,
thoughts that were real.
I loved you for moving me forward,
loving what I did.

You taught me how to be patient,
how not to rush love.
You taught me to put love,
in front of my insecurities.
You taught me,
the path to truly love.

I learned to love you,
unconditionally.
I learned to love myself,
to love you more sincerely.
I learned to work harder,
when you worked tirelessly.

I knew you had a quick temper;
I calmed you down with patience.
I knew you loved to read,
I wrote you a poem a day each.
I knew you were not much of a romantic;
I was your hopeless romantic.

You rarely get butterflies;
you felt it in my cuddles under the rain.
You knew we had faults and flaws,
we moved through thick and thin.
You felt we had a future;
butterflies came alive in my heart.

I wanted to grow and bond,
only with you.
I wanted mutual happiness towards eternal love,
always with you.
I wanted to be in that special place in your heart,
like you did.

This was a promise I wrote for dear you.

When you put
a promise out
in the universe,
make sure you
mean it and own it.

Even if a
promise may
be unpredictable,
make sure you
try realising it
with conviction.

Breathe
love,
believing
in
love.

sharlene
word Yourstory
2016

You can't see love.
Breathe it, feel it, just like air.

Sharlene Leong
Born 1980

GREEN LIGHT

Your face lit up,
behind the birthday candles.
You wore a sleek shirt;
there came my adrenaline rush.
The impression of you,
stuck with me like an angel.

I asked to be connected,
was told to be careful.
Couldn't resist the temptation,
I revolved myself around you.
Excited to see me,
happy I was always there for you.

We grew closer,
chatted through every night.
I bought supper for you,
just because you were hungry.
A kiss a night,
after each walked in the park.

We fell deep,
into the dreams of wonder.
You were so pure,
someone so precious.
On cloud nine,
never once apart.

Expressions of love
were never needed.
Feelings of love
were always present.
Affections of love
were stimulated.

In a whole new world,
you pushed me to express my feelings.
I finally did,
in a whole different language.
Before we could conclude,
you said, "We'll talk tomorrow".

Why gave me the green light,
yet asked for a sudden break?
Why said you really liked me,
yet asked for distance?
Why did you stop me,
yet asked for expressions?

Be sure to
speak the truth
when you want to
hear the truth.

Be ready to
receive the truth
when you ask
for the truth.

sharlene
worldYourstory
2016

Nothing beats authenticity.

Sharlene Leong
Born 1980

EMBRACE AS ONE

Be part of each other's lives.
Be there.
Be present.

Not only about work but also about life.

Connect on a deeper sense,
not only on the surface.

Know everything and anything.

Be open.

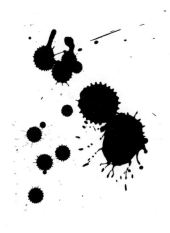

Always
grow together through
thick and thin.

Always
lovingly embrace
as one.

EVERLASTING LOVE

Hide,
to understand.

Distance,
to stir curiosity.

Avoid eye contact,
to breathe normally.

Romance,
to excite love.

Remember,
to pray.

Surrender,
to let go.

Slow down,
to await true love.

Allow love,
to spread its wings.

Do not rush,
to say I love you.

When you embrace imperfection,
it leads to everlasting love.

DREAMS

The place we called home, from a crazy day.
I hugged you tight, drained the stress away.
I stretched my hands out, embraced your fall.

The beautiful smile arose, as I nibbled your ears.
I missed you much; there I cuddled you with love.
I snuggled you up, to plant a perfect kiss.

The rain came, I cozied you.
I tucked you in, protected from the gusty wind.
I blanketed you close, kept you warm.

The moon and stars, I picked for you.
I looked at the sky at night; I brought the stars to you.
I looked at your reflection, I found upon the moon.

The day you had intense pain, I took care of you.
I meant so much to you, when I cared for your well-being.
I was always there for you, every time you needed me.

The day all that was different was beautiful.
I couldn't see, the things felt with the heart.
I chose to believe, and I chose to have faith.

The day you broke my heart, tears reached my cheeks.
I cried myself to sleep; I woke with a heavy heart.
I had a special place in your heart,
so I kept myself there.

The strength within, through the difficult embrace.
I asked to stay; yet you asked me to leave.
I wanted communication, yet you gave up easily.

The confusion arose, with tons of emotions.
I was told, I was yours but I couldn't hear from you.
I was told, you were mine but I couldn't see you.

The struggles never came the rested mind.
I wished so much to hear from you, but I never did.
I wanted so much to be part of your life,
but you got annoyed.

The day I dreamt, you were my other half.
I held you so close, yet you seemed so far away.
I had a bittersweet taste, thoughts of you resurfaced.

Let all true feelings
be retained as real.

Don't fight it.

Being happy doesn't mean
all departments
of your life
have to be perfect.

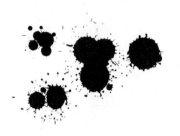

Don't be attached
to something easily detectable.

Breathe the dreams
for your next adventure.

charlene
wordYourStory
2016

Embrace the imperfection that you once try to make perfect.

Sharlene Leong
Born 1980

YOUR CHOICE

Trying to impress someone can only last so long.
Touch them with sincerity.

You know someone is making use of you,
detach from that toxicity.
Look into genuine distractions.

One shall never be attached to another
just because you feel alone.
Be attached to yourself.

Put things into perspective,
you will see the direction you need to take.

Have the courage
to step away from toxicity,
even if that is
the last option you have.

Make new true possibilities.

DESIRE

Every desire comes with a price.

Having the desire to know?
Respect the truth that doesn't want to be told.

The uncertainties always linger on.
It unknowingly and knowingly runs wild.

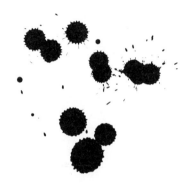

Do you know it is the mysterious that
causes the effects of wanting to know?

Though you want to know,
stop the energy that you feed on in circles.

Even if intuition kicks in,
you will still yearn to know from other sources.

IMAGINE releasing the energy to know,
you will eventually realise there isn't a need to know.

sharlene
word Yourstory
2016

Enjoy the journey of the unknown.

Sharlene Leong
Born 1980

MOVING IN CIRCLES

Knowing
how the world moves in circles.

Surprisingly
how memories are filled.

Romantically
how we grow closer.

Amazing
how life revolves around us.

Believing
how change is inevitable.

Adapting
how we are presented.

Treasuring
how moments never last.

Trusting
how time unfolds.

Like it or not,
we are always moving in circles.

FAITH

You came for a reason.
Serving a purpose,
teaching a lesson.

Who are you?
The look into your eyes,
I always figured.

There will be discovery,
through pain,
through sorrow,
through anxiety.
These are reflections of the mind.

There will be realisation,
through motivation,
through strength,
through love,
These are willingness of the heart.

You came for a reason.
Nothing happens without a reason.

The illness,
the injury,
the lost,
the stupidity,
these test the safety of the directionless soul.

The determination,
the independence,
the focus,
the freewill,
these test the limits of the soul.

Successes and downfalls,
these are the important messages.

Whatever it really is,
have faith unconditionally.

Successes and downfalls through life never end.

sharlene
wordYourstory
2016

Choose to have faith unconditionally.

Sharlene Leong
Born 1980

BUT

I wanted to chat with you,
but I had neither courage nor energy to.

You cried and were stressed out,
but just what could I do?

I experienced the worst,
but you weren't even there.

I typed you letters,
but they weren't even sent.

We celebrated Christmas,
but once would never be enough.

I had a gift for you,
but you would never receive it.

You had a gift for me,
but I would never receive it.

Isn't it easier to decide upon
what is and what is not?

Leave the 'buts' behind,
experience it and be with it.

Being in-between black and white,
it is gray,
which might be worst.

TWO STEPS BACK

Don't be the third party,
you will hurt everyone involve.
How sure are you,
there will not be a forth party?

If it is meant to be,
something magical will happen.
Don't force your way into any relationship.
Don't play tricks to gain trust.
Trust base on tricks, won't last.

Obsession never works;
you will only scare your partner away.
Give them space to miss you,
to grow fonder.
When you know you have gone overboard,
take two steps back.
You will see a brighter future together.

Seeing
everything
from afar,
helps
see a
brighter future
together.

STRANGE LOVE

Two worlds collided, where destiny brought us together.
You found me; there I fell for you.
This must be love.

I fell so fast, felt you were the one.
I went all out, tried to know all about you.
I thought I did, but I never knew.

I was sure, I didn't need reasons to love you.
I held tightly onto you, thought I would lose you.
I never understood why, you chose to part ways.

I broke down, as you drifted away.
I struggled, for your dear return.
I saw the light, at our reunion.

I felt your emotions, which slowed everything down.
I enjoyed the process, I realised why I loved you.
I saw the warmth, which was burning slow.

You said you really liked me, you said it was true.
You loved what I wrote for you, yet faded away.
You came along, but were so far away.

You acted strange, the way you communicated.
You couldn't provide answers, like lovers could.
You left me hanging, like we never were.

I thought beauty was needed, aesthetics being all.
I was always drawn, to the temple.
I had always, missed the light within.

I couldn't understand you better, I never did.
I chose to believe, but I needed so much proof.
I blocked off all emotions, just to send you love.

You felt my presence, my deepest desires.
You heard what I said, but were never listening.
You shut me off, like you never would.

You never really know
what lies behind
the spoken words.

Just breathe
and let it breathe,
no matter what
you think you know.

Listen
to your soul,
with your
deepest persuasion.

One day,
it doesn't
even matter.

A LOVE NOTE

A love note a day,
keeps the smiles going strong.

I wake up feeling tired,
but missing you keeps me wide-awake.

I plant a kiss on your forehead,
and whisper a sweet soft morning dear.

I write a beautiful note,
to serenade your sweet soul today.

THE MOON

Upon the moon,
your lovely reflection,
butterflies flutter in my heart.

Butterflies glow,
a hopeless romantic,
kisses in your heart.

Lovely kisses pass the moon,
landing on dear you.

Loving dear you,
sleep missing you,
awake thinking of you.

sharlene
wordYourstory
2016

Butterflies don't come easy.
Don't lose it for you felt it.

Sharlene Leong
Born 1980

DO YOU REALLY KNOW?

You are special,
so special in my heart.
You shine bright,
so bright within my heart.
You are the one,
the one that lives inside my heart.

Do you know everything feels like yesterday?
Do you know I get lost in you?
Do you know I have searched for you among so many stars?

Why ask me not to ignore the bad feelings,
and cause it on purpose?
Why am I so patient,
or are you still teaching me how to be patient?
Why don't you know,
you are still the one I'm waiting for?

Do you know I hope you want to see me too?
Do you know,
how I really feel?

Do you really know?

Be mentally prepared in order to receive.

Be ready in order to commit.

Be strong in order to be weak.

Be independent in order not to be reliant.

SUFFER

Saying no can save heartaches after.

Don't stay in a relationship
for the sick of it.

It is better to end it early
than suffer much more lately.

BE HONEST

Start with friendship,
build that foundation,
and see both sides of the story.

Love blossoms,
let it breathe,
the heart will stay with you.

Be honest,
sooner or later,
you will know.

LINGERS ON

Lingering;
so dangerous these emotions are.
Witnessing;
so real these movements are.

Experiencing;
so surreal these distances are.
Faking;
so honest these truths are.

Erasing;
so strong these memories are.
Imagining;
so pointless these thoughts are.

Missing;
so romantic these expressions are.
Loving;
so poetic these lovers are.

Believing;
so suspicious these proofs are.
Knowing;
so aware these secrets are.

Hearing;
so loud these voices are.
Wishing;
so strong these desires are.

FOUNDATION

Sweet surprises
are always sweet,
but that shall not be
the basic foundation.

You need
to establish love
with concrete devotion,
which will survive
any earthquake.

LOVE

Love is simple, yet complicates.
Love shall be learned, yet tiring.
Love sets rules, yet messes up.

Is Love at first sight right?
Is Love real or pretentious?
Is Love present at the initial stage?

Can lust turn into Love?
Can true feelings evolve?
Can you really understand Love?

The gut, it mixes with emotions.
The flow, it shows complexity.

Love is original, yet duplicates.
Love is agreeable, yet straining.
Love sets rules, yet resists rules.

Is Love mainly a four-letter word?
Is Love connective?
Is Love the only track to follow?

Can life be without Love we crave?
Can there be a bed of roses in Love?
Can you really have enough Love?

The feeling of love, it may be right.
The experience of love, it can be wisdom.

We are always learning how to love.
What is love is basically what love is.

PRESENCE

On a dear photo,
I found a smile so sweet.
Imagine you near,
holding you close.

Accidental fate,
destiny meets.
So much patience,
so little time.

Living by yourself,
do live well.
Look at the sky,
dream of my presence.

A butterfly flutters;
it is I nearby.
Don't feel insecure;
believe me I am here.

LET BE

Let live.
Let go.
Let life.

Let God.
Let us embrace.
Let you and I.

Let love.
Let us be free.

Let all be kind.
Let us be wise.

Let the music play.
Let the rhythm flow.
Let us run wild.

Let imagination be your eyes.
Let movement be movement.
Let energy flow.

Let the memories breathe.
Let be.

Do
everything
with
love.

There
is
no
tomorrow.

Sharlene leong
has a passion for design,
a love for words,
as music is an essential.

She deals with graphic and advertising,
and leans towards the arts and design,
breathing words into her stories.

Here are other original artworks
of the legendary and the remembered:

Find more of her stories, designs,
artworks and contacts at
wordyourstory.com
facebook.com/wordyourstory
instagram.com/wordyourstory